THE MODERN ENTERPRISE ARCHITECT

A New Era, a New Purpose, a New Approach

Paul Gadbois

MODERN ENTERPRISE PRESS

The Modern Enterprise Architect: A New Era, A New Purpose, A New Approach

Copyright © 2026 Paul Gadbois

All rights reserved.

ISBN: 979-8-9952235-1-1

First Edition

Published by

South Carolina, USA

Content:

Introduction:

What exactly is an Enterprise Architect, and what should they be doing for the business?

Ask a hundred executives that question, and you'll probably get a hundred different answers. Ask a hundred Enterprise Architects, and you'll get just as many.

So why is there so much confusion and inconsistency? I see three main reasons:

1. The business capability known as Enterprise Architecture contains multiple layers of architects—each with a distinct focus and purpose. Most people don't realize this and tend to view "architecture" as a one-size-fits-all discipline.

2. Many existing enterprise architecture frameworks don't clearly explain or differentiate these layers for business leaders and architects.

3. These frameworks tend to stay theoretical, offering little practical guidance for actually standing up a real, functioning architecture practice.

So, what does a well-defined architecture practice look like when the layers are clearly defined?

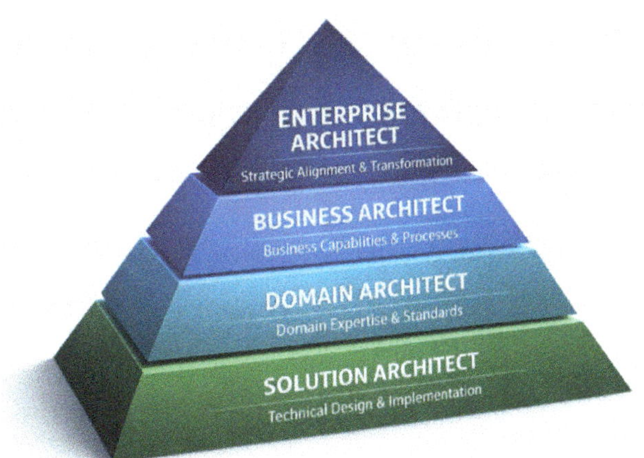

Figure 1-Enterprise Architecture Layers

The Enterprise Architect

Aligns business strategy with technology execution. Translates strategic goals into objectives, objectives into critical success factors, critical success factors into required business capabilities, target-state architectures, and multi-year transformation roadmaps. The focus: enterprise-wide optimization, value realization, and business transformation—not individual solutions.

The Business Architect

Models how the business operates—its capabilities, value streams, organizational structures, and operating model. Ensures the business strategy is executable and structurally sound before technology solutions are applied. Connects strategy to tangible execution.

The Domain Architect (or Segment Architect)

Defines architecture standards and direction within a functional or technology area (for example, Data, Applications, Infrastructure, Security, or Integration). Builds the patterns, guardrails, and reference architectures that ensure consistency and quality across solutions.

The Solution Architect

Designs the architecture for a specific initiative or project. Integrates components from various domains to deliver a complete, working solution that aligns with enterprise and domain standards. The focus here is on a defined project scope, not the entire enterprise.

The solution layer is what most people typically think of when they hear the term *enterprise architecture*. While this layer does deliver some business value, its impact is limited without the added benefits provided by the three layers above it.

Leaders often picture Enterprise Architects as purely technical experts—focused on infrastructure, applications, data, or security. In reality, Enterprise Architects operate at a much more strategic level. We bridge business goals with actionable objectives, define critical success factors, and identify the business capabilities needed to reach them. When business leaders embrace this distinction, Enterprise Architects can drive transformation—not just technology. The real value is realized when leadership empowers the Enterprise Architects to help shape the organization's future.

This book marks the beginning of a new era for Enterprise Architecture—one driven by a new purpose and a new approach. It challenges the long-standing misconception that Enterprise Architects exist primarily as deep technical specialists and establishes their role at the strategic center of the organization. *The Modern Enterprise Architect* reveals how today's architects translate business ambition into structured execution, connecting goals to objectives, success factors, and the capabilities needed to deliver meaningful outcomes. By elevating architecture beyond the technology stack, this new approach unlocks greater business value, sharper clarity, and sustained transformation. Ultimately, this book is a practical guide for leaders and practitioners embracing a new purpose for Enterprise Architecture—one that empowers organizations to adapt, evolve, and drive future success.

Setting the stage: why aligning tech to strategy is make-or-break.

Organizations today are not short on vision. Executive teams routinely craft bold strategic statements, articulate ambitious growth targets, and publish inspiring mission narratives. Yet despite this clarity of intent, many organizations struggle to translate vision into measurable outcomes. The gap between aspiration and execution remains one of the most persistent challenges in modern enterprises. The reason is rarely a lack of intelligence, effort, or even resources. More often, it is the absence of a disciplined roadmap that connects strategy to reality.

Vision without a roadmap is direction without traction.

At the highest level, strategy defines *where* an organization wants to go. It reflects leadership's understanding of market forces, competitive positioning, and long-term priorities. However, strategy by itself is inherently abstract. Phrases such as "improve customer experience," "drive digital transformation," or "increase operational efficiency" are directionally correct but operationally incomplete. They describe intent but not execution.

This is where many organizations begin to drift. Leaders assume that once strategy is communicated, the organization will naturally align and move forward. In practice, the opposite often occurs. Different departments interpret the same strategic statement in different ways. Technology teams launch initiatives that seem aligned but lack measurable business impact. Investments accumulate, but outcomes remain inconsistent.

What is missing is the structured translation layer between vision and delivery.

A roadmap provides that translation.

A well-constructed strategic roadmap decomposes high-level ambition into a sequence of actionable elements. It begins by clarifying strategic objectives in measurable terms. Objectives then inform the critical success factors that must be achieved. Those success factors, in turn, reveal the business capabilities the organization must strengthen or build. Only after these capabilities are clearly understood should technology solutions enter the conversation.

This order of operations is essential.

Many organizations invert the process. They begin with technology initiatives and attempt to map them upward to strategy after the fact. This creates what might be called "technology gravity," where delivery teams become busy implementing tools, platforms, and systems that may be technically sound but strategically disconnected. The result is familiar: fragmented investments, duplicated capabilities, and mounting complexity without proportional business value.

A roadmap pre'

When properly designed, every technology initiative can be traced upward to a business capability, every capability to a critical success factor, and every success factor to a strategic objective. This creates organizational clarity. It allows leadership to answer fundamental questions with confidence:

- Why are we doing this initiative?

- What business outcome does it support?

- How does it advance our strategy?

Without this line of sight, organizations operate largely on momentum and assumption.

Another critical function of the roadmap is prioritization. Strategy typically produces more potential work than the organization has capacity to execute. Without a structured roadmap, prioritization becomes political rather than analytical. The loudest voice, the most urgent fire, or the most visible executive sponsor often determines what moves forward.

A capability-driven roadmap changes the conversation. Instead of debating projects in isolation, leadership can evaluate which capabilities most directly advance strategic objectives. Investments become portfolio decisions rather than individual project approvals. This shift dramatically improves capital efficiency and organizational focus.

Equally important is the roadmap's role in sequencing.

Transformation is rarely achieved through a single initiative. It requires coordinated movement across people, process, data, and technology. Certain capabilities must mature before others can succeed. Foundational data work, for example, often precedes advanced analytics. Integration maturity frequently enables customer experience improvements. Without deliberate sequencing, organizations attempt to build upper floors before the foundation is stable.

The roadmap makes dependencies visible.

It articulates where the organization must build first, where it can accelerate, and where it must be patient. This visibility reduces execution risk and prevents the costly rework that occurs when initiatives are launched out of order.

While solution and domain architects focus on how systems are designed and implemented, the Enterprise Architect operates at the strategic translation layer. Their role is not merely to design technology landscapes but to ensure that business intent, capability evolution, and technology investment move in deliberate alignment. They provide the connective tissue between executive ambition and operational reality.

Unfortunately, many organizations underutilize this role.

When Enterprise Architects are pulled too deeply into solution delivery, their ability to shape the roadmap diminishes. They become reviewers of technology decisions rather than orchestrators of enterprise direction. The organization loses the very perspective needed to maintain strategic coherence across a complex portfolio of initiatives.

Elevating the roadmap discipline restores that balance.

It positions Enterprise Architecture where it is most valuable—at the intersection of strategy, capability planning, and investment alignment. It enables leadership to move from reactive project funding to intentional transformation management.

In today's environment of constant disruption, this capability is no longer optional. Markets shift quickly. Technology cycles compress. Customer expectations evolve continuously. Organizations that rely on ad hoc execution models struggle to keep pace. Those that institutionalize roadmap-driven strategy execution create a repeatable mechanism for turning vision into measurable progress.

The difference is not merely operational—it is competitive.

Organizations that consistently translate strategy into coordinated action build momentum. They reduce waste, accelerate time to value, and create organizational confidence in their ability to execute change. Over time, this becomes a defining capability.

In the end, strategy is not proven by the elegance of its language but by the evidence of its outcomes. Vision sets the direction, but the architectural roadmap makes the journey possible. Without it, even the most compelling strategy risks remaining aspirational. With it, organizations gain the clarity, discipline, and alignment required to move from vision to reality.

Identifying the must-wins that drive your mission.

Every organization sets goals. Strategic plans are drafted, vision statements are refined, and leadership teams articulate where the enterprise intends to go. Yet despite this clarity of intent, many organizations struggle to consistently achieve the outcomes they envision. The gap rarely exists at the level of ambition—it exists in the translation layer between goals and execution. This is precisely where Critical Success Factors (CSFs) become indispensable.

If strategy defines the destination, Critical Success Factors define the conditions that must be true for the organization to arrive there.

Too often, organizations move directly from high-level goals into initiatives, projects, and technology investments. While well intentioned, this shortcut introduces significant risk. Without clearly defined success conditions, teams may deliver activity without producing impact. Projects can finish on time and on budget while still failing to materially advance the strategic objective they were meant to support.

Critical Success Factors provide the discipline that prevents this drift.

A CSF is not simply another metric or performance indicator. It is a focused statement of what must go right for a strategic objective to succeed. Where goals express *what* the organization wants to achieve, CSFs clarify *what must be true* to make achievement possible. They narrow the aperture, forcing leadership to identify the few conditions that truly determine success.

This distinction matters.

Consider a common strategic goal: improving customer experience. Without further refinement, this goal is directionally sound but operationally vague. Different parts of the organization may interpret it differently. Marketing may focus on personalization. Operations may focus on service speed. Technology teams may invest in new platforms. Each effort may be valuable, but without alignment around the true drivers of success, the organization risks fragmentation.

By defining Critical Success Factors, the organization sharpens its focus. Leadership may determine that success depends on three conditions: unified customer data, consistent cross-channel engagement, and reduced service response time. These CSFs now act as the organization's GPS signals. They provide clarity about what must improve and where investment should concentrate.

The power of CSFs lies in their ability to drive alignment.

When clearly articulated, they create a shared understanding across business and technology teams. They help answer questions that frequently stall transformation efforts:

- What matters most right now?

- Where should we focus our limited resources?

- How will we know if our strategy is actually working?

Without CSFs, prioritization often becomes reactive and fragmented. With them, decision-making becomes intentional and evidence-based.

Equally important is the role CSFs play in connecting strategy to business capabilities. Once success factors are identified, the next logical question emerges: what must the organization be able to do—consistently and at scale—to satisfy these conditions? This is where capability thinking enters the picture.

For example, if a CSF requires unified customer data, the organization must possess strong capabilities in data integration, master data management, and data governance. If rapid service response is critical, capabilities in case management, workflow automation, and knowledge management may need to mature.

This progression—from goal to CSF to capability—creates architectural clarity. It ensures that investments are not driven by technology trends but by business necessity. Technology becomes an enabler of clearly defined success conditions rather than the starting point of the conversation.

This is the essence of the Goal GPS™ Framework.

The Goal GPS™ Framework

A structured method for translating strategic goals into measurable execution through Critical Success Factors and enabling capabilities.

Just as a navigation system continuously guides a traveler toward a destination, CSFs guide the organization toward strategic outcomes. They provide course correction when initiatives drift. They illuminate gaps in organizational maturity. They enable leadership to monitor whether progress is truly advancing the mission or merely generating activity.

However, defining effective Critical Success Factors requires discipline. Not every important activity qualifies as a CSF. If everything is critical, nothing is. Strong CSFs share several characteristics.

First, they are tightly linked to strategic objectives. A CSF must clearly influence whether the goal succeeds or fails. If the connection is weak or indirect, the factor is likely a supporting activity rather than a true success driver.

Second, they are few in number. Most objectives should have only a small handful of CSFs. This scarcity creates focus. It forces leadership to make intentional choices about what matters most.

Third, they are actionable. A well-formed CSF points the organization toward capability development and measurable improvement. It should be clear what the enterprise must strengthen in order to satisfy the condition.

Fourth, they are outcome-oriented. CSFs describe states of organizational effectiveness, not just the completion of tasks. "Implement a new CRM system" is not a CSF. "Achieve a unified customer view across channels" is.

When organizations apply this rigor, the benefits compound quickly. Strategic conversations become more precise. Investment portfolios become more coherent. Architecture roadmaps gain sharper direction. Most importantly, execution becomes measurably tied to business outcomes.

Because Enterprise Architects operate at the intersection of strategy, capability, and technology, they are uniquely positioned to facilitate CSF definition. They help leadership move beyond aspirational language into operational clarity. They ensure that each success factor can be traced forward into capability requirements and ultimately into enabling technologies.

Without this architectural discipline, CSFs risk becoming another layer of documentation. With it, they become powerful instruments of transformation.

In today's environment of rapid change, organizations cannot afford misalignment between strategy and execution. Markets move too quickly. Technology evolves too rapidly. Resource constraints grow tighter each year. The enterprises that succeed are those that navigate with precision.

Critical Success Factors provide that precision.

They transform strategy from a static statement into a dynamic guidance system. They illuminate what truly matters. They focus investment where it will produce the greatest impact. And they create the traceability required to move confidently from vision to measurable results.

In the end, defining goals is only the beginning. The organizations that consistently win are those that understand the deeper question: what must be true for this strategy to succeed? When leadership answers that question with clarity and discipline—and empowers the Modern Enterprise Architect to guide the translation—the path forward becomes far more navigable. The Modern Enterprise Architect ensures that ambition is converted into structured, traceable execution. That is the power of the Goal GPS™ Framework—and why defining your Critical Success Factors, under strong architectural leadership, is one of the most important strategic capabilities an organization can develop.

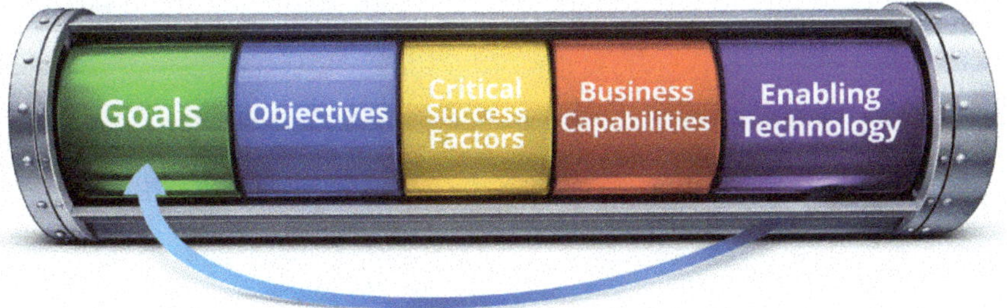

Figure 3 - The Goal GPS™ Strategy Pipeline

Breaking down the core business capabilities needed to succeed.

If strategy defines where an organization intends to go, and Critical Success Factors clarify what must be true to succeed, then business capabilities answer the most operationally important question of all: what must the organization actually be able to do—reliably and at scale—to deliver on its strategy?

This is the moment where strategy stops being aspirational and starts becoming executable.

Many organizations struggle at this stage because they jump too quickly into projects, systems, or organizational changes without first defining the underlying capabilities required for success. The result is familiar: initiatives proliferate, technology investments multiply, and transformation programs consume significant resources—yet the organization sees only incremental progress toward its strategic goals.

The missing ingredient is almost always capability clarity.

A business capability describes what the organization must be able to perform, independent of how it is currently implemented. It is stable even as processes, organizational structures, and technologies evolve. Capabilities such as customer onboarding, donor stewardship, risk management, data integration, or service case resolution represent enduring organizational competencies. They define what the business does, not how it happens today.

This distinction is critical.

Processes change. Systems get replaced. Organizational charts are redrawn. But the fundamental capabilities required to operate and compete remain relatively constant. By focusing on capabilities, leaders create a durable blueprint for transformation—one that survives technology cycles and organizational reshuffling.

Capabilities function as the true building blocks of execution.

Once Critical Success Factors have been defined, the next logical step is to identify which capabilities must mature or be developed to satisfy those success conditions. For example, if a strategic objective requires a highly personalized customer experience, the organization may need stronger capabilities in customer data management, journey orchestration, analytics-driven decisioning, and cross-channel engagement. If operational efficiency is the goal, capabilities such as process automation, workflow management, and performance monitoring may become priority focus areas.

This business capability lens introduces precision into strategic planning.

Instead of launching broad, loosely connected initiatives, leadership can target specific capability gaps. Investment decisions become grounded in measurable organizational needs rather than technology trends or vendor influence. This shift alone dramatically improves the return on transformation spending.

Capability modeling also creates a shared language across the enterprise.

One of the persistent challenges in large organizations is semantic misalignment. Business leaders speak in terms of outcomes and services. Technology teams speak in terms of systems and platforms. Finance speaks in terms of investments and cost centers. Without a common abstraction layer, strategic conversations often devolve into translation exercises.

Capabilities solve this problem elegantly.

Because they describe what the business must do—without prescribing how—they provide a neutral, cross-functional vocabulary. Business stakeholders can validate whether the right capabilities are being prioritized. Technology teams can map systems and solutions to capability enablement. Finance leaders can align funding to capability maturity rather than isolated projects. The result is a far more coherent planning and governance model.

Operating above individual solutions but below pure strategy, the Enterprise Architect is uniquely positioned to define, model, and govern the organization's capability landscape. They ensure that capabilities are clearly articulated, properly decomposed, and consistently mapped to both strategic objectives and enabling technologies. Most importantly, they maintain the traceability that allows leadership to understand exactly how investments are advancing enterprise priorities.

Without this architectural discipline, capability discussions often become academic exercises. With it, capabilities become actionable instruments of transformation.

Another important advantage of capability-based planning is sequencing.

Not all capabilities can or should be matured simultaneously. Some serve as foundational enablers for others. For example, advanced analytics capabilities typically depend on strong data management foundations. Digital experience improvements often require prior investments in integration and identity management. Attempting to advance higher-order capabilities without strengthening the underlying layers leads to predictable failure and costly rework.

A well-constructed capability roadmap makes these dependencies visible.

It allows leadership to sequence investments logically, balancing quick wins with foundational work. It also provides a mechanism for measuring progress over time. Capability maturity models—whether simple or sophisticated—enable organizations to assess current state, define target state, and track improvement in a structured way.

This visibility is particularly valuable in complex transformation environments, where multiple initiatives compete for attention and funding.

However, capability modeling must be approached with discipline. One common pitfall is over-engineering the capability map. Organizations sometimes create excessively granular models that are difficult to maintain and nearly impossible for executives to consume. The goal is not architectural perfection; it is strategic clarity.

Effective capability maps typically share several characteristics.

They are hierarchical but not overly deep. They reflect the organization's operating model. They are stable over time. And most importantly, they are actively used in planning, governance, and investment decisions. A capability model that lives only in a slide deck delivers little value. One that becomes embedded in portfolio management and strategic planning becomes a powerful decision instrument.

Another frequent mistake is treating capabilities as purely a technology exercise.

Business capabilities encompass people, process, data, and technology working together to produce an outcome.

While technology often enables capability improvement, capabilities themselves are business constructs. They encompass people, process, data, and technology working together to produce an outcome. Organizations that focus only on system implementation while neglecting operating model changes often find that capability maturity stalls despite significant technology investment.

True capability building is holistic.

It requires alignment across organizational design, process optimization, data quality, governance, and technology enablement. This is why capability-based planning is so effective: it forces leaders to think beyond systems and consider the full operating model required for success.

In an era of continuous disruption, this discipline is becoming increasingly important. Organizations can no longer afford transformation efforts that produce activity without measurable advancement of strategic priorities. They need a structured way to translate ambition into organizational muscle.

Business capabilities provide that muscle.

They represent the repeatable competencies that allow strategy to become reality. When clearly defined, properly prioritized, and actively governed, they create a durable foundation for sustained performance and adaptability.

In the end, successful organizations do not simply launch initiatives—they deliberately build the capabilities required to win. By treating capabilities as the true building blocks of execution, and by empowering the Modern Enterprise Architect to guide their evolution, leaders create a far more reliable path from strategy to outcomes. This is what your organization needs to do—and why capability building must sit at the heart of modern enterprise transformation.

How to choose tech that moves the needle.

If business capabilities define what an organization must be able to do, then technology defines how effectively—and how efficiently—it can do it at scale. Yet despite decades of digital investment, many organizations still struggle to realize the full value of their technology portfolios. Systems are implemented, platforms are upgraded, and new tools are continuously introduced, but measurable business impact often lags expectations.

The root cause is rarely technical failure. More often, it is architectural misalignment.

Too many organizations treat technology selection as the starting point of transformation rather than its enabling layer. Vendors promise innovation, project teams rush to implement solutions, and roadmaps become tool-centric rather than outcome-driven. When this happens, technology begins to pull the organization instead of the organization deliberately directing technology. The result is a familiar pattern: fragmented platforms, overlapping functionality, rising costs, and growing complexity.

The enterprise must counter this drift by embracing a "rules before tools" philosophy—anchoring technology decisions in modern architectural principles.

Matching technology to capability is the discipline that restores order and intentionality to the digital landscape. It ensures that every major technology investment can be clearly traced to the business capabilities it enables and, ultimately, to the strategic objectives the organization is trying to achieve. This traceability is the difference between technology that accumulates and technology that transforms.

At its core, the technology-to-capability connection is about sequencing the right conversations in the right order.

Strategy defines where the organization wants to go. Critical Success Factors clarify what must be true for success. Business capabilities define what the organization must be able to do. Only then should technology enter the discussion as the mechanism that enables capability maturity (Rules before tools). When organizations reverse this order, they inevitably end up optimizing systems instead of advancing outcomes.

Consider a common scenario. An organization decides it needs a new customer relationship management (CRM) platform. The selection process begins with feature comparisons, vendor demonstrations, and implementation timelines. Yet often missing from the conversation is a clear articulation of the capabilities the organization is trying to improve. Is the goal to enhance customer insight? Improve pipeline visibility? Enable omnichannel engagement? Strengthen relationship management workflows?

Without this clarity, even the most sophisticated platform can underperform expectations.

When capability needs are explicitly defined first, technology decisions become far more precise. The organization can evaluate whether a platform genuinely strengthens the targeted capability or merely adds incremental functionality. Implementation scope becomes clearer. Integration priorities become more obvious. Most importantly, success metrics become measurable in business terms rather than technical ones.

This is the essence of architectural discipline.

The Modern Enterprise Architect plays a pivotal role in maintaining this discipline. Positioned between business strategy and technical execution, the Enterprise Architect ensures that technology investments are neither ad hoc nor purely reactive. Instead, they are deliberately aligned to the organization's capability roadmap.

This alignment begins with mapping.

Each major business capability should have a clear view of the technologies that enable it. In some cases, a single platform may support multiple capabilities. In others, a capability may depend on a coordinated set of applications, data services, and integration layers. The goal is not to force one-to-one relationships but to establish transparent line-of-sight between capability needs and technology assets.

Once this visibility exists, several powerful governance benefits emerge.

First, redundancy becomes easier to detect. Many organizations unknowingly fund multiple tools that support the same capability. A capability-based technology map quickly reveals these overlaps, creating opportunities for rationalization and cost optimization.

Second, gaps become visible. Leadership can see where critical capabilities lack sufficient technological support. This helps prioritize investment in areas that directly affect strategic outcomes rather than spreading resources thinly across marginal improvements.

Third, modernization efforts gain focus. Instead of launching broad "digital transformation" initiatives, organizations can target specific capability enablement opportunities. This reduces risk and accelerates time to value.

However, matching technology to capability is not a one-time exercise. Both business needs and technology landscapes evolve continuously. New platforms emerge. Legacy systems age. Strategic priorities shift. The connection between capability and technology must therefore be actively governed over time.

This is where many organizations fall short.

They may conduct an architecture review during a major transformation initiative, but they fail to institutionalize the practice. Over time, project-level decisions begin to erode alignment. Tactical exceptions accumulate.

Shadow IT emerges. Gradually, the architecture drifts away from the original strategic intent.

Effective organizations embed this discipline into portfolio governance, solution review processes, and investment planning. They require that new technology proposals clearly state which capabilities they enable and how success will be measured. They periodically review capability maturity alongside technology performance. And they empower Enterprise Architecture to act not merely as a review function but as a strategic partner in investment decision-making.

Another important dimension of this work is recognizing that technology alone does not create capability maturity.

This is a critical point that is often misunderstood.

While technology can dramatically accelerate capability performance, true capability strength also depends on process design, data quality, organizational alignment, and workforce readiness. A new platform implemented on top of broken processes or poor data will rarely deliver its promised value. Matching technology to capability therefore requires a holistic perspective.

The Modern Enterprise Architect must continually ask not just, "Do we have the right technology?" but also, "Is the operating model ready to fully leverage it?" This broader lens distinguishes architecture-led transformation from tool-driven modernization.

In today's environment, where technology options continue to proliferate at an unprecedented pace, this discipline becomes even more important. Cloud platforms, AI capabilities, automation tools, and specialized applications offer enormous potential—but also significant risk of fragmentation if adopted without architectural intent.

Organizations that master the tech connection gain a significant competitive advantage. Their technology portfolios remain lean but powerful. Their investments produce measurable business outcomes. Their transformation efforts compound rather than conflict. And their leadership teams gain confidence that digital spending is directly advancing strategic priorities.

In the end, technology should never be the starting point of enterprise change. It should be the precision instrument that enables clearly defined business capabilities to perform at their highest potential. By rigorously matching technology to capability—and by empowering the Modern Enterprise Architect to govern that alignment—organizations create a far more disciplined, transparent, and effective path from digital investment to business value.

Building a step-by-step roadmap that's both strategic and practical.

Strategy may define the destination, and capabilities may define what the organization must be able to do, but without a well-crafted roadmap, even the most compelling strategy will struggle to gain traction. Execution does not happen by aspiration alone—it happens through deliberate sequencing, disciplined prioritization, and visible progress over time. This is the art and science of roadmap craftsmanship.

Too often, organizations treat roadmaps as simple project timelines or static planning documents. They become crowded Gantt charts filled with overlapping initiatives, optimistic delivery dates, and loosely connected workstreams. While these artifacts may provide activity visibility, they rarely provide strategic clarity. A true enterprise roadmap is not merely a schedule—it is a strategic navigation instrument.

At its best, a roadmap answers three critical questions: What must we do first? What must come next? And how do today's investments move us measurably closer to our target state?

This is where many organizations struggle.

In the absence of strong architectural discipline, initiatives often emerge from multiple directions at once. Business units propose enhancements. Technology teams advocate for platform upgrades. Compliance introduces new requirements. Innovation groups pursue emerging opportunities. Each initiative may be individually justified, but collectively they can create a fragmented and resource-constrained environment where progress feels busy but unfocused.

Roadmap craftsmanship brings order to this complexity.

The starting point for any effective roadmap is traceability. Every major work effort should connect back to a defined business capability and, ultimately, to a strategic objective or Critical Success Factor. This ensures that the roadmap reflects intentional movement toward enterprise priorities rather than a collection of disconnected projects.

The Modern Enterprise Architect plays a central role in establishing this traceability. By maintaining line-of-sight from strategy through capabilities to enabling technologies, the architect ensures that roadmap decisions are grounded in business value. This perspective elevates the roadmap from an IT planning artifact to an enterprise decision framework.

Once traceability is established, sequencing becomes the next critical discipline.

Not all initiatives can or should begin simultaneously. Many capabilities have natural dependency relationships. Foundational data capabilities often must mature before advanced analytics can deliver value. Integration layers typically must be strengthened before digital experience improvements can scale effectively. Security and identity services frequently underpin broader platform modernization efforts.

A well-crafted roadmap makes these dependencies explicit.

Rather than forcing parallel progress where logical sequencing is required, the roadmap should reflect a deliberate progression of capability maturity. This sequencing does not necessarily slow transformation—it often accelerates it by reducing rework, minimizing architectural & technical debt, and ensuring that each phase builds upon a stable foundation.

Another hallmark of roadmap craftsmanship is horizon-based planning.

Effective roadmaps typically operate across multiple time horizons. Near-term initiatives focus on immediate value delivery and foundational improvements. Mid-term efforts expand and scale capabilities. Long-term investments position the organization for future differentiation and innovation. By structuring the roadmap across horizons, leadership gains both short-term momentum and long-term direction.

This multi-horizon view also helps balance competing executive pressures. Organizations often feel tension between delivering quick wins and investing in foundational capabilities that may take longer to mature. A well-designed roadmap makes both visible, allowing leadership to intentionally manage the trade-offs rather than react to them.

Equally important is the concept of roadmap realism.

One of the most common failure patterns in transformation efforts is overcommitment. Roadmaps become overly ambitious, assuming unlimited capacity, perfect execution, and static business conditions. When reality inevitably intervenes—through resource constraints, shifting priorities, or unforeseen complexity—confidence in the roadmap begins to erode.

Roadmap craftsmanship requires intellectual honesty.

Capacity constraints must be acknowledged. Organizational readiness must be assessed. Technology dependencies must be validated. The goal is not to produce the most aggressive roadmap—it is to produce the most credible one. Credibility builds executive trust, and trust sustains long-term transformation momentum.

Another dimension of effective roadmap design is adaptability.

No roadmap survives unchanged over multiple years. Market conditions evolve. Regulatory environments shift. Strategic priorities are refined. Emerging technologies create new opportunities. The roadmap must therefore function as a living instrument rather than a fixed contract.

The Modern Enterprise Architect again plays a vital stewardship role here. By continuously monitoring capability maturity, technology performance, and strategic alignment, the architect helps leadership adjust the roadmap without losing directional integrity. This balance—structured yet flexible—is what distinguishes mature transformation organizations from reactive ones.

Communication is another often underestimated aspect of roadmap craftsmanship.

A technically perfect roadmap that executives cannot easily interpret will fail to influence decision-making. Visual clarity, narrative coherence, and executive-level framing are essential. Leadership should be able to quickly see how investments connect to strategic priorities, where major milestones lie, and how risk is being managed.

This is why leading organizations often maintain multiple roadmap views: an executive summary view for leadership alignment, a capability view for architectural governance, and a delivery view for program execution teams. Each serves a different audience while preserving a single underlying source of truth.

Finally, roadmap craftsmanship requires governance discipline.

Without ongoing oversight, even well-designed roadmaps can drift. Tactical exceptions accumulate. Urgent requests bypass prioritization processes. Over time, the carefully sequenced plan begins to fragment. Effective organizations establish governance mechanisms that require new initiatives to demonstrate alignment with capability priorities before entering the roadmap. This protects strategic focus while still allowing for necessary agility.

In today's environment of accelerating change, roadmap discipline has become a defining organizational competency. Technology cycles are shorter. Business expectations are higher. Resource constraints are tighter. Organizations that treat roadmaps as static planning artifacts will struggle to keep pace. Those that elevate roadmap craftsmanship into a core architectural practice gain a powerful execution advantage.

In the end, plotting the course is not about predicting the future with perfect precision. It is about creating a structured, transparent, and adaptable path from current state to strategic ambition. When roadmap craftsmanship is done well—grounded in capability logic, sequenced with discipline, and governed with intent—the organization moves forward with clarity and confidence.

This is how strategy becomes momentum. And it is why the Modern Enterprise Architect must stand at the center of the roadmap conversation, ensuring that every step forward is both deliberate and aligned to the enterprise's long-term destination.

Turning plans into action across the organization.

A well-crafted roadmap is a powerful instrument. It brings clarity to strategy, sequences investments logically, and aligns stakeholders around a shared destination. Yet many organizations discover a hard truth after the applause fades from the roadmap presentation: planning momentum does not automatically translate into execution progress. The difference between organizations that admire their roadmaps and those that realize value from them lies in disciplined execution.

Execution is where strategy earns its credibility.

Across industries, leadership teams invest significant energy in building compelling strategic narratives and visually impressive roadmaps. But too often, the roadmap becomes a static artifact—a document presented once, admired briefly, and then gradually overshadowed by day-to-day operational pressures. Initiatives begin to drift, priorities compete for attention, and the original sequencing logic starts to erode.

This is the execution gap.

Bridging that gap requires more than project management rigor. It demands architectural stewardship, governance discipline, and sustained leadership alignment. The Modern Enterprise Architect plays a pivotal role in ensuring that the roadmap evolves from presentation material into a living execution engine.

The first requirement for effective roadmap execution is operational ownership.

A roadmap cannot succeed if it lives solely within the strategy or architecture function. Each major initiative must have clear business ownership, defined accountability, and measurable success criteria tied directly to the capabilities it is intended to advance. When ownership is ambiguous, progress slows and accountability diffuses. When ownership is explicit, momentum accelerates.

However, ownership alone is not sufficient.

Execution also requires maintaining the traceability that made the roadmap valuable in the first place. As initiatives move into delivery phases, there is a natural tendency for teams to focus narrowly on scope, timelines, and technical challenges. While necessary, this project-level focus can gradually disconnect work from its strategic intent. Over time, the organization risks completing projects successfully while falling short of its broader transformation goals.

This is where the Modern Enterprise Architect must remain actively engaged.

Rather than stepping away after the roadmap is approved, the architect serves as the connective tissue between strategy and delivery. They continuously validate that initiatives remain aligned to the capabilities and Critical Success Factors they were designed to support. They monitor for scope drift that could dilute business impact. And they help leadership understand when emerging realities require roadmap adjustments.

In mature organizations, this function is embedded within portfolio governance.

Effective portfolio governance ensures that new work entering the pipeline demonstrates clear alignment to capability priorities. It also provides structured checkpoints to assess whether in-flight initiatives are delivering the expected value. Without this discipline, even well-designed roadmaps can slowly fragment under the weight of tactical pressures.

Another critical dimension of execution is capacity realism.

One of the most common execution failures stems from overcommitment. Organizations often approve more initiatives than their people, funding, or change capacity can realistically support. Early in the roadmap lifecycle, this may not be obvious. But as delivery teams begin to compete for shared resources—data engineers, integration specialists, security reviewers, business subject matter experts—bottlenecks emerge.

Roadmap execution must therefore be grounded in honest capacity planning.

The Modern Enterprise Architect, working closely with portfolio and delivery leaders, helps ensure that sequencing reflects not only logical dependencies but also organizational readiness. This includes technology readiness, data maturity, process stability, and workforce capability. When these factors are ignored, transformation efforts frequently stall despite strong strategic intent.

Equally important is the role of measurement.

Execution without measurement quickly becomes activity without insight.

Organizations must define, upfront, how capability improvement will be assessed. This does not mean relying solely on traditional project metrics such as schedule adherence or budget performance. While important, those indicators measure delivery efficiency—not business impact.

True execution discipline requires capability-level metrics.

For example, if a roadmap initiative aims to strengthen customer onboarding, leadership should track cycle time reduction, error rates, customer satisfaction, or conversion improvements. If the objective is to enhance data-driven decision making, metrics might include data quality scores, analytics adoption rates, or decision latency reduction.

These measures keep execution tethered to outcomes.

They also create a powerful feedback loop. When leaders can see which capabilities are genuinely improving, they can adjust investment priorities with greater confidence. This transforms the roadmap from a static plan into a dynamic learning system.

Communication is another often underestimated execution lever.

During roadmap development, alignment tends to be high because stakeholders are deeply engaged in planning discussions. But as execution unfolds over months and years, attention naturally shifts. New priorities emerge. Leadership changes occur. Organizational memory fades. Without deliberate communication rhythms, even well-aligned organizations can lose sight of the roadmap's intent.

High-performing organizations establish regular roadmap reviews at the executive level.

These sessions do not merely report project status. They focus on capability progress, risk exposure, and strategic alignment. The Modern Enterprise Architect often facilitates these conversations, helping leadership interpret complex delivery signals through a strategic lens.

Flexibility also plays a crucial role.

Execution discipline should not be confused with rigidity. Markets change. Regulatory pressures evolve. Technology opportunities emerge. A roadmap must be stable enough to guide action but flexible enough to adapt when conditions warrant.

The key is governed adaptability—not reactive volatility.

The Enterprise Architect again serves as a stabilizing force. By continuously monitoring the relationship between strategy, capabilities, and technology investments, the architect helps leadership make informed adjustments without losing directional coherence.

Ultimately, successful execution requires cultural reinforcement.

Organizations that consistently translate roadmaps into progress share a common mindset: they treat architecture and roadmap discipline as core management capabilities, not one-time planning exercises. Leaders ask regularly how current work advances strategic capabilities. Investment discussions reference the roadmap as the primary decision framework. Delivery teams understand the business outcomes their work is meant to enable.

When this cultural alignment takes hold, execution accelerates naturally.

In the end, the journey from presentation to progress is where enterprise transformation either gains momentum or quietly stalls. A roadmap, no matter how elegant, delivers value only when it is actively governed, realistically sequenced, and relentlessly aligned to business capability improvement. By empowering the Modern Enterprise Architect to steward this process—and by embedding execution discipline into the fabric of the organization—leaders can ensure that their roadmap becomes what it was always meant to be: a living engine of measurable progress.

How to keep your roadmap flexible as your organization evolves.

If there is one certainty in modern enterprise environments, it is this: change is constant. Markets evolve, technologies advance, regulatory landscapes shift, and organizational priorities inevitably adjust. Yet many organizations continue to treat their strategic roadmaps as if they were static contracts rather than dynamic navigation instruments. The result is predictable. Plans grow stale, initiatives lose alignment, and transformation momentum begins to fade.

A roadmap that cannot adapt will eventually become irrelevant.

This is why the concept of the *living roadmap* has become so essential to modern enterprise success. A living roadmap is not a document that is periodically revisited; it is an actively governed, continuously informed, and strategically responsive instrument that evolves alongside the organization it serves. It preserves directional integrity while enabling necessary course corrections. Most importantly, it ensures that strategy remains connected to reality over time.

The need for adaptability begins with a simple truth: no organization operates in a static environment.

Even the most carefully constructed roadmap is based on assumptions—about market conditions, technology trajectories, resource availability, and organizational readiness. Over time, some of those assumptions will inevitably change. New competitive pressures may emerge. A regulatory requirement may accelerate a previously low-priority capability. A merger or leadership shift may introduce new strategic objectives. Emerging technologies such as AI or automation may create opportunities that did not exist when the roadmap was first developed.

Organizations that treat their roadmap as fixed often struggle when these shifts occur. They face a difficult choice between rigid adherence to an outdated plan or reactive abandonment of carefully sequenced work. Neither outcome supports sustained transformation.

The living roadmap offers a more disciplined alternative.

Rather than discarding structure in the name of agility, the living roadmap embeds adaptability into the governance model itself. It establishes regular review cadences, defined decision triggers, and clear ownership for monitoring strategic alignment. This allows leadership to adjust direction deliberately rather than reactively.

The Modern Enterprise Architect plays a central role in enabling this adaptability.

Positioned at the intersection of strategy, capability planning, and technology enablement, the Enterprise Architect maintains continuous visibility into how the organization is progressing toward its target state. They monitor capability maturity trends, technology performance, emerging risks, and external market signals. When conditions begin to diverge from original assumptions, the architect helps leadership interpret what those signals mean and whether roadmap adjustments are warranted.

This is not about constant change for its own sake.

A living roadmap balances stability and flexibility. Stability provides organizational confidence and protects against thrashing. Flexibility ensures relevance in the face of real-world change. The discipline lies in knowing when to hold the course and when to adjust.

One of the most effective mechanisms for maintaining a living roadmap is the establishment of structured review horizons.

High-performing organizations typically review roadmap progress across multiple timeframes. Near-term initiatives are monitored closely for delivery risk and capability impact. Mid-term investments are reassessed for sequencing validity and dependency health. Long-term strategic bets are periodically evaluated against evolving market conditions. This multi-horizon perspective prevents surprises and enables proactive course correction.

Another critical element of the living roadmap is feedback integration.

Execution generates data—about delivery velocity, capability improvement, user adoption, and business impact. Organizations that treat this data as a learning asset gain a significant advantage. Rather than waiting for annual planning cycles, they use execution feedback to continuously refine roadmap priorities.

For example, if a capability improvement initiative is delivering faster-than-expected value, leadership may choose to accelerate related investments. Conversely, if adoption is lagging despite successful system implementation, the roadmap may need to incorporate additional process or organizational change work. The key is to treat the roadmap as a hypothesis that is continuously validated through execution evidence.

Governance discipline is what makes this sustainable.

Without clear governance, the concept of a living roadmap can devolve into uncontrolled change. Tactical requests begin to bypass prioritization. Urgent demands crowd out strategic work. Over time, the roadmap loses coherence. Mature organizations avoid this trap by establishing formal change criteria. New initiatives must demonstrate alignment to strategic objectives and capability priorities before entering the roadmap. Adjustments are made through structured review forums rather than ad hoc escalation.

The Modern Enterprise Architect often serves as the steward of this governance model.

By maintaining the traceability from strategy to capabilities to enabling technologies, the architect ensures that roadmap changes remain intentional and evidence-based. They help leadership understand the downstream implications of sequencing changes. They highlight where new work may introduce architectural risk or resource contention. In doing so, they preserve both agility and architectural integrity.

Another often overlooked aspect of the living roadmap is communication continuity.

Roadmaps do not fail only because of poor planning; they often fail because organizational alignment erodes over time. Leadership attention shifts. New executives bring different priorities. Delivery teams focus on immediate milestones. Without deliberate communication rhythms, the shared understanding that existed during roadmap approval begins to fragment.

Organizations that succeed with living roadmaps maintain regular executive-level roadmap reviews. These sessions focus not just on project status but on capability progress, risk posture, and strategic alignment. Visual clarity is critical. Leaders should be able to quickly see how the roadmap is evolving and why adjustments are being made. Transparency builds trust, and trust sustains long-term transformation.

Cultural mindset also plays a significant role.

In organizations where roadmaps are viewed as static commitments, any change can be perceived as failure or instability. In organizations that embrace the living roadmap philosophy, adaptation is understood as a sign of strategic maturity. Leaders recognize that disciplined adjustment is not course correction born of confusion—it is navigation informed by new intelligence.

This mindset shift is subtle but powerful.

It transforms the roadmap from a one-time planning deliverable into an enduring management capability. It encourages evidence-based decision-making. It reinforces cross-functional alignment. And it enables the organization to move forward with both confidence and responsiveness.

In today's environment of accelerating change, this capability is no longer optional. The pace of technological innovation, market disruption, and organizational complexity continues to increase. Static planning models cannot keep up. Organizations that cling to rigid roadmaps risk falling behind even when their original strategy was sound.

In the end, adapting to change is not about abandoning structure—it is about strengthening it with feedback, governance, and architectural insight. By treating the roadmap as a living instrument and by empowering the Modern Enterprise Architect to steward its evolution, organizations create a transformation capability that is both disciplined and resilient. This is how strategy remains relevant, execution stays aligned, and the enterprise continues moving forward—even as the landscape around it evolves.

Making sure everyone—from executives to frontline managers—can leverage the roadmap.

A roadmap is only as powerful as the organization's ability to execute it. While much attention is rightly placed on strategic clarity and architectural rigor, the ultimate success of any enterprise roadmap depends on something more human and more dynamic: leadership at every level of the organization. Without distributed ownership and empowered teams, even the most elegant roadmap will struggle to translate intent into sustained progress.

Too often, roadmaps are treated as executive artifacts—documents owned by senior leadership, reviewed in boardrooms, and communicated downward as directional guidance. While executive sponsorship is essential, this top-heavy model creates a dangerous gap between strategy and execution. Teams may understand what the organization is trying to achieve but lack the context, authority, or confidence to act decisively in support of it.

Empowerment closes that gap.

When leadership is activated at every level—executive, managerial, and frontline—the roadmap becomes more than a plan. It becomes a shared operating framework that guides decision-making across the enterprise. Individuals understand not just what they are doing, but why it matters and how their work contributes to broader strategic outcomes.

This alignment is what transforms activity into momentum.

The first step in enabling leadership at every level is clarity. Teams cannot execute against ambiguity. They must be able to see how their work connects to business capabilities, Critical Success Factors, and strategic goals. This is where the Modern Enterprise Architect plays a foundational role. By maintaining clear traceability from strategy to capability to technology, the Enterprise Architect provides the connective tissue that makes the roadmap intelligible across organizational layers.

When done well, this traceability answers the questions teams naturally ask:

- How does this initiative support the organization's priorities?

- What capability are we trying to improve?

- How will success be measured?

Without these answers, teams often default to local optimization— delivering what is immediately in front of them rather than what most advances enterprise outcomes.

However, clarity alone is not enough. Empowerment also requires decision rights.

In many organizations, teams are expected to execute rapidly but must navigate layers of approval to make even modest adjustments. This creates friction, slows delivery, and discourages initiative. A roadmap-driven organization must deliberately define where decisions can be made locally and where architectural guardrails must be maintained centrally.

This balance is critical.

Too much central control creates bottlenecks and suppresses innovation. Too little governance leads to fragmentation and architectural drift. The Modern Enterprise Architect helps calibrate this balance by establishing clear design principles, reference architectures, and capability priorities that provide teams with freedom inside well-defined boundaries.

Within these guardrails, teams can move with confidence.

Another essential element of leadership at every level is capability ownership. Roadmaps often fail when capabilities are treated as abstract concepts rather than managed assets. High-performing organizations assign explicit ownership for key capabilities, typically at the business leadership level. These capability owners are accountable not only for current performance but for maturity progression over time.

This ownership model creates powerful alignment.

When a leader is accountable for improving, for example, customer onboarding capability, roadmap initiatives become more than project milestones—they become instruments of measurable business improvement. Capability owners partner with delivery teams, architects, and technology leaders to ensure that investments produce real operational gains.

This shared accountability reinforces the roadmap's relevance across the organization.

Communication rhythm also plays a decisive role in sustaining empowered execution. Roadmaps should not be communicated once and assumed to be understood indefinitely. Organizational attention shifts quickly. New hires join. Priorities evolve. Without ongoing reinforcement, even well-aligned teams can lose sight of the roadmap's intent.

Effective organizations establish regular forums where roadmap progress is reviewed through a capability lens. These sessions focus not just on delivery status but on business impact and alignment. The Modern Enterprise Architect often facilitates these discussions, helping translate complex delivery signals into strategic insights that resonate with both executives and operational leaders.

Many teams are accustomed to working within project plans but have limited exposure to capability-based thinking. Helping managers and delivery leads understand how to interpret the roadmap—and how their work fits within it—significantly increases execution coherence. Training, visual models, and consistent language all contribute to this literacy.

When teams begin to think in terms of capability progression rather than isolated deliverables, their decision-making naturally improves.

Cultural reinforcement further amplifies this effect. Organizations that succeed with roadmap-driven transformation embed the roadmap into everyday management conversations. Investment discussions reference capability priorities. Quarterly reviews assess progress against roadmap horizons. Performance objectives incorporate measurable contributions to capability maturity.

The Modern Enterprise Architect again serves as a key enabler of this cultural shift. By consistently framing decisions in terms of capability impact and strategic alignment, the architect helps leadership reinforce the behaviors that sustain roadmap momentum. They ensure that architectural thinking is not confined to planning cycles but is continuously reflected in execution decisions.

Adaptability must also be built into the empowerment model.

As discussed in the concept of the living roadmap, conditions will change. New priorities will emerge. Teams must be equipped not only to follow the roadmap but to signal when adjustments may be necessary. Empowered teams provide valuable ground-level intelligence about delivery friction, capability gaps, and emerging opportunities. Organizations that create safe pathways for this feedback gain a significant advantage.

This does not mean the roadmap becomes fluid or undisciplined. Rather, it becomes informed by real execution data from across the enterprise. Leadership at every level contributes to both progress and learning.

In the end, the success of any roadmap is not determined solely by its strategic elegance or architectural precision. It is determined by whether the organization can mobilize its people around it. When teams understand the roadmap, trust its direction, and have the authority to act within its guardrails, execution accelerates naturally.

This is the power of leadership at every level.

By empowering teams with clear traceability, defined decision boundaries, capability ownership, and continuous communication, organizations transform the roadmap from a planning artifact into a shared engine of progress. And by positioning the Modern Enterprise Architect as the steward of alignment across these layers, leaders ensure that strategy remains connected to execution in a way that is both disciplined and dynamic.

When this alignment takes hold, the roadmap does more than guide the enterprise forward—it enables every level of the organization to actively participate in shaping the journey.

Defining metrics to make sure your roadmap delivers results.

A roadmap without measurement is little more than an informed guess. Organizations may feel confident in their strategic direction, energized by their transformation initiatives, and encouraged by visible activity across the enterprise. But without disciplined measurement, leadership cannot know whether the organization is truly progressing toward its intended outcomes. Activity can be mistaken for impact, and motion can be mistaken for momentum.

Measuring what matters is the discipline that separates hopeful execution from accountable transformation.

In many organizations, performance measurement remains heavily focused on traditional project metrics—on-time delivery, budget adherence, and scope completion. While these indicators are useful for managing delivery efficiency, they are insufficient for evaluating roadmap success. Projects can be delivered perfectly from a project management perspective and still fail to produce meaningful business improvement.

The fundamental question is not simply, "Did we deliver?" It is, "Did capability performance measurably improve in a way that advances our strategy?"

This shift in perspective is essential.

A roadmap exists to drive strategic outcomes through capability maturation. Measurement must therefore be anchored at the capability level. Each major roadmap initiative should have clearly defined success indicators that reflect real-world business impact. These indicators provide leadership with an objective view of whether the organization is moving closer to its target state.

The Modern Enterprise Architect plays a critical role in establishing this measurement discipline.

Because the architect maintains traceability from strategy to Critical Success Factors to business capabilities and enabling technologies, they are uniquely positioned to define meaningful performance indicators. They help ensure that metrics are not selected simply because they are easy to capture, but because they genuinely reflect progress toward strategic objectives.

This is where many measurement efforts falter.

Organizations often default to what might be called "convenience metrics"—data points that are readily available in existing dashboards but only loosely connected to business outcomes. System uptime, ticket closure rates, or feature release counts may provide useful operational insight, but they rarely tell leadership whether the enterprise is becoming more capable in ways that matter strategically.

Capability-aligned metrics provide far greater clarity.

For example, if the roadmap prioritizes improving customer onboarding capability, meaningful measures might include onboarding cycle time, first-contact resolution rate, customer satisfaction during onboarding, or conversion rates from initial engagement to active customer status. If the focus is on strengthening data-driven decision making, metrics might include data quality scores, analytics adoption rates, decision latency reduction, or forecast accuracy.

These measures connect execution to enterprise value.

Another important dimension of measuring roadmap success is establishing baselines. Before capability improvement can be assessed, the organization must understand its current performance level. Too often, initiatives launch without a clear baseline, making it difficult to quantify

improvement later. Establishing a credible current-state assessment—
however imperfect—creates the reference point necessary for meaningful
progress tracking.

From there, organizations can define target-state aspirations.

Maturity models are particularly useful in this context. Whether formal or
lightweight, capability maturity models allow leadership to assess where
the organization stands today and where it intends to be over time. They
also provide a structured way to sequence investments and track
incremental advancement. The Modern Enterprise Architect typically helps
design and maintain these maturity frameworks, ensuring they remain
aligned to strategic priorities.

---

*"Did capability performance measurably improve in a
way that advances our strategy?"*

However, measurement must extend beyond individual capabilities.

At the portfolio level, leadership needs visibility into whether the roadmap
as a whole is delivering the intended strategic impact. This requires a
balanced measurement model that incorporates multiple dimensions of
performance. Leading organizations often monitor progress across four key
lenses:

First, capability performance—are targeted capabilities actually improving?

Second, delivery effectiveness—are initiatives being executed with
reasonable efficiency and predictability?

Third, business outcomes—are improvements translating into measurable
financial, customer, or operational gains?

Fourth, architectural health—are technology investments reducing
complexity, improving integration, and strengthening the overall technology
posture?

This multidimensional view prevents over-optimization in any single area.

For example, an organization might deliver initiatives quickly but create
architectural debt that slows future innovation. Alternatively, it might
improve certain operational metrics while failing to move the needle on

customer experience or revenue growth. Balanced measurement helps leadership detect these patterns early.

Another critical factor in successful measurement is cadence.

Metrics must be reviewed regularly enough to inform decisions but not so frequently that the organization becomes reactive to short-term noise. Most mature organizations establish a rhythm of monthly operational reviews, quarterly capability assessments, and semiannual strategic evaluations. This layered cadence allows for both tactical responsiveness and strategic perspective.

The living roadmap depends on this feedback loop.

As discussed in earlier chapters, the roadmap must remain adaptable to changing conditions. Measurement provides the evidence base that informs when adjustments are warranted. If capability improvement is lagging despite strong delivery performance, leadership may need to reassess process design, organizational readiness, or data quality. If certain initiatives are producing outsized impact, the roadmap may warrant acceleration in related areas.

Without measurement, these insights remain invisible.

Transparency also plays an essential role in sustaining measurement discipline. Metrics should not live solely within executive dashboards. Capability owners, delivery teams, and business leaders should have visibility into how their work contributes to broader roadmap success. This shared visibility reinforces accountability and strengthens alignment across organizational layers.

The Modern Enterprise Architect often helps curate this transparency by translating complex performance data into executive-friendly visualizations. Heatmaps, capability scorecards, and roadmap progress views allow leadership to quickly interpret where progress is strong and where attention is needed.

Cultural mindset again proves decisive.

Organizations that view measurement as a compliance exercise tend to collect large volumes of data with limited impact on decision-making. High-performing organizations treat measurement as a strategic management tool. Leaders actively use capability metrics to inform investment decisions, adjust sequencing, and validate whether transformation efforts are delivering real value.

This mindset shift turns metrics into instruments of learning rather than mere reporting artifacts.

In today's environment of rapid change and constrained resources, measuring what matters is no longer optional. Technology investments continue to grow in scale and complexity. Stakeholder expectations continue to rise. Boards and executive teams increasingly demand evidence that transformation spending is producing tangible outcomes.

Organizations that cannot demonstrate this linkage risk losing both credibility and momentum.

In the end, roadmap success is not defined by how many initiatives are launched or how many systems are implemented. It is defined by whether the organization becomes measurably more capable in ways that advance its strategic goals. By anchoring measurement at the capability level, maintaining disciplined baselines and targets, and empowering the Modern Enterprise Architect to steward performance visibility, leaders create a powerful feedback system that keeps strategy, execution, and outcomes tightly aligned. This is how organizations move beyond activity tracking and begin truly measuring what matters.

Reflections on how roadmaps shape long-term organizational impact.

Every organization builds plans. Many build strategies. Some even construct detailed roadmaps. But only a few leaders recognize the deeper truth: a well-crafted roadmap is not merely a planning artifact—it is a leadership legacy in motion.

Long after individual projects are completed and specific technologies are replaced, the discipline an organization develops around strategic alignment, capability building, and execution coherence continues to shape its trajectory. This is why the roadmap, when done right, becomes far more than a delivery tool. It becomes an enduring management capability that outlives any single initiative, platform, or leadership tenure.

Your roadmap is ultimately a reflection of how your organization chooses to move forward.

Too often, roadmaps are treated as temporary planning exercises tied to annual budgeting cycles or major transformation programs. They are built with urgency, presented with confidence, and then gradually allowed to decay as new priorities emerge. When this happens, organizations fall back into reactive patterns—funding disconnected initiatives, chasing emerging technologies without clear business alignment, and struggling to maintain architectural coherence.

This cycle erodes momentum and institutional confidence.

Leaders who think in terms of legacy take a different approach. They recognize that the true value of roadmap discipline lies in the operating muscle it builds inside the enterprise. A living, capability-driven roadmap creates repeatable clarity. It teaches the organization how to translate strategy into structured execution. It embeds traceability into decision-making. And it establishes governance patterns that persist even as specific business conditions evolve.

In this sense, the roadmap becomes part of the organization's DNA.

The Modern Enterprise Architect plays a pivotal role in shaping this legacy. Positioned at the intersection of strategy, capability planning, and technology enablement, the architect ensures that roadmap thinking is not confined to a single transformation wave. Instead, it becomes an enduring enterprise competency. Through consistent modeling, governance, and communication, the architect helps leadership institutionalize the behaviors that sustain long-term alignment.

This work is both technical and cultural.

Technically, the roadmap provides structured visibility into where the organization is today and where it intends to go. It sequences investments logically. It highlights dependencies. It surfaces risk. But culturally, the roadmap reinforces a mindset of intentional progress. It encourages leaders at every level to ask the most important question: how does this decision move us closer to our strategic destination?

When this mindset takes hold, decision quality improves across the enterprise.

Investment discussions become more disciplined. Technology selections become more purposeful. Transformation initiatives become more coherent. Over time, the organization develops a reputation—not just for ambition—but for execution credibility. This credibility is one of the most valuable legacies any leadership team can leave behind.

Another defining characteristic of roadmap legacy is resilience.

Markets will change. Leadership will turn over. Technology platforms will evolve. But organizations that have embedded capability-based roadmap discipline are far better equipped to navigate these transitions. Because their planning model is grounded in business capabilities rather than specific tools or organizational structures, they can adapt without losing strategic coherence.

This is the power of thinking beyond the current planning horizon.

Leaders who focus only on near-term delivery often optimize for immediate wins at the expense of long-term adaptability. In contrast, leaders who build roadmap discipline as a core enterprise capability create a foundation that future teams can build upon. They reduce the likelihood of architectural drift. They minimize redundant investments. And they provide future decision-makers with a clear line of sight into why the enterprise operates the way it does.

Your roadmap becomes the institutional memory of your strategic intent.

However, legacy is not created through documentation alone. It is created through sustained behavioral reinforcement. Organizations must continue to use the roadmap as the primary lens for investment decisions, capability prioritization, and transformation sequencing. The Modern Enterprise Architect often serves as the steward of this continuity, ensuring that roadmap thinking remains embedded in governance forums and executive conversations.

Communication plays an equally important role.

For a roadmap to become part of the organizational legacy, it must be visible, understandable, and trusted. Leaders must regularly reinforce how current initiatives connect to capability priorities. Teams must see how their work contributes to measurable progress. Executives must be able to quickly interpret where the organization stands relative to its target state.

Transparency builds confidence. Confidence sustains momentum.

Over time, the roadmap begins to shape organizational behavior in subtle but powerful ways. Teams become more proactive in identifying capability gaps. Business leaders become more disciplined in articulating outcomes before requesting technology investments. Portfolio discussions become more evidence-based. The enterprise shifts from reactive modernization to intentional evolution.

This is when the roadmap transcends its original purpose.

It becomes not just a guide for what the organization is doing, but a signal of how the organization thinks. It reflects a commitment to clarity over complexity, alignment over fragmentation, and outcomes over activity. These are the hallmarks of mature, high-performing enterprises.

Of course, building this kind of legacy requires persistence. Roadmap discipline must be maintained through leadership transitions, budget pressures, and competing priorities. There will always be pressure to accelerate individual initiatives outside the established sequence. There will always be new technologies promising rapid transformation. The organizations that preserve their roadmap integrity are those that balance responsiveness with architectural discipline.

They understand that legacy is built through consistency.

In the end, every leadership team leaves something behind. Some leave a collection of disconnected systems and partially completed initiatives. Others leave a coherent operating model that future leaders can confidently extend. The difference lies in whether roadmap discipline was treated as a temporary planning exercise or as a foundational enterprise capability.

Your roadmap is your opportunity to shape that outcome.

By grounding it in business capabilities, governing it with architectural rigor, measuring it with meaningful metrics, and empowering teams to execute against it, you create far more than a plan. You create a durable framework for sustained enterprise progress.

That is the true promise of the Modern Enterprise Architect—and the enduring impact of roadmap craftsmanship done well. When leaders embrace this perspective, the roadmap becomes more than a path forward. It becomes a legacy of clarity, alignment, and intentional transformation that continues to guide the organization long after the original journey began.

Bringing It All Together:

Across these ten chapters, a clear and disciplined narrative has emerged: Enterprise Architecture, when properly understood and applied, is not about technology diagrams—it is about enabling organizations to move from intention to impact with precision and confidence.

We began by establishing the critical bridge between strategy and execution, then introduced the Goal GPS™ Framework as the structured method for translating ambition into actionable clarity. From there, we explored the essential building blocks of capability definition, the deliberate matching of technology to business need, and the craftsmanship required to plot a credible, sequenced roadmap. We examined what it takes to execute that roadmap in the real world, how to keep it alive in the face of constant change, and how to empower leadership at every level to carry the strategy forward. Finally, we addressed the importance of measuring what truly matters and recognized the enduring legacy that disciplined roadmap thinking creates.

Threaded through every chapter is the evolving role of the Modern Enterprise Architect.

No longer confined to technical oversight, the Modern Enterprise Architect operates as the strategic translator, capability orchestrator, and alignment steward for the enterprise. By maintaining traceability from goals to outcomes, governing technology with intent, and enabling informed decision-making across the organization, this role ensures that strategy does not remain aspirational—it becomes operational.

In the end, the organizations that thrive will be those that elevate Enterprise Architecture to this modern standard, transforming it from a technical function into a core engine of sustained, strategic progress.

Onward,
Paul Gadbois

Appendix A - Goal GPS™ Framework Summary

The Goal GPS™ Framework provides a disciplined, traceable method for translating enterprise strategy into measurable execution. It ensures that technology and investment decisions remain firmly anchored to business outcomes.

Figure 4 - Goal GPS™ Framework Summary

At its core, the framework answers five essential questions in sequence:

1. Goals — Where are we going?
Strategic goals define the enterprise's intended direction. These should be few in number, outcome-focused, and clearly articulated by leadership.

2. Objectives — What specifically must we achieve?
Objectives break strategic goals into measurable targets. They establish clarity around success criteria and time horizons.

3. Critical Success Factors (CSFs) — What must be true for success?
CSFs identify the conditions that must exist for objectives to be realized. They represent the make-or-break elements of execution.

4. Business Capabilities — What must the organization be able to do?
Capabilities translate CSFs into operational competencies. They are stable, business-centric constructs independent of specific processes or systems.

5. Technology Enablement — How do we support and scale performance?
Technology is mapped last, ensuring investments directly strengthen priority capabilities rather than driving them.

When applied consistently, the Goal GPS™ Framework creates:

- clear strategic traceability

- disciplined investment alignment

- reduced technology sprawl

- improved execution confidence

The Modern Enterprise Architect serves as the steward of this framework, maintaining alignment across all layers as the organization evolves.

Appendix B - Capability Definition Template

Business Capability Definition Template

Use this template to standardize capability modeling across the enterprise.

Capability Name

(Clear, business-oriented label)

Example: Donor Relationship Management

Capability Description

(What the organization must be able to do — not how)

Provide a concise description of the business outcome this capability enables.

Business Owner

(Accountable executive or function)

Identifies who is responsible for capability performance and maturity.

Strategic Alignment

Supported Goals/Objectives:
List the strategic elements this capability enables.

Current Maturity Level

Figure 5 - Capability Maturity Model

Use a simple 1–5 scale:

1 — Initial / Ad hoc
2 — Emerging
3 — Defined
4 — Managed
5 — Optimized

Target Maturity Level

Define the desired state aligned to roadmap horizons.

Key Performance Indicators (KPIs)

Examples:

- cycle time

- quality/error rate

- customer satisfaction

- throughput

* cost efficiency

KPIs should measure business performance, not system activity.

Enabling Technologies

List major platforms that support this capability.

Known Gaps / Risks

Document constraints, dependencies, or performance issues.

Appendix C - Enterprise Roadmap Review Checklist

Use this checklist during roadmap development and quarterly reviews.

Strategic Alignment

- ☐ Does each initiative map to a defined business capability?
- ☐ Is there clear linkage to goals and objectives?
- ☐ Are Critical Success Factors explicitly addressed?

Sequencing Discipline

- ☐ Are foundational capabilities prioritized first?
- ☐ Are major dependencies identified and respected?
- ☐ Is the roadmap realistic given organizational capacity?

Investment Focus

- ☐ Are there overlapping or redundant technology investments?
- ☐ Do investments strengthen priority capabilities?
- ☐ Is technical debt being actively reduced?

Execution Readiness

- ☐ Are business owners clearly assigned?
- ☐ Are success metrics defined at the capability level?
- ☐ Is change management considered where required?

Architectural Integrity

- ☐ Does the roadmap reduce fragmentation?
- ☐ Are integration and data implications addressed?

- • ☐ Does the plan support long-term scalability?

Living Roadmap Discipline

- • ☐ Is there a defined review cadence?

- • ☐ Are feedback loops incorporated?

- • ☐ Can the roadmap adapt without losing coherence?

Appendix D - Key Terms and Definitions

Business Capability

What the organization must be able to do to execute its strategy.
Independent of specific processes or systems.

Critical Success Factor (CSF)

A condition that must be true for a strategic objective to succeed.

Enterprise Architecture (EA)

The discipline that aligns business strategy, operating model, and
technology to enable coherent enterprise execution.

Goal GPS™ Framework

A structured method for translating goals into objectives, CSFs,
capabilities, and enabling technology.

Modern Enterprise Architect

A strategic translator and alignment steward who connects business intent
to execution reality across the enterprise.

Roadmap

A sequenced, capability-aligned plan that guides the organization from
current state to target state.

Technology Enablement

The application of platforms, tools, and data services to strengthen
business capability performance.

Traceability

The ability to follow the logical connection from strategy through execution artifacts.

62

About the Author

Paul Gadbois is a technology executive, enterprise strategist, and author whose career has focused on helping organizations align technology, data, and operational capabilities with mission-driven outcomes. Throughout his career, he has served in senior leadership roles including Chief Technology Officer and Senior Enterprise Architect, guiding organizations through complex initiatives involving digital transformation, enterprise architecture, and technology modernization.

Recognized as a technology scholar and strategic thinker, Gadbois has spent decades working at the intersection of business strategy, organizational change, and technology innovation. His work emphasizes the importance of aligning enterprise architecture with real-world business objectives, enabling organizations to move beyond traditional IT models toward more integrated, outcome-focused operating environments.

A prolific author on topics including technology management, cybersecurity, and business resource management, Gadbois has written eighteen previous books in the technology and leadership domain. *The Modern Enterprise Architect: A New Era, A New Purpose, A New Approach* represents his nineteenth publication and reflects his evolving perspective on the future role of enterprise architecture in modern organizations.

For consulting or speaking inquiries related to the Goal GPS™ Framework, the Goal GPS™ Strategy Pipeline, and Modern Enterprise Architecture, please contact Paul Gadbois at:

paul@paulgadbois.com

www.ingramcontent.com/pod-product-compliance
Lightning Source LLC
Chambersburg PA
CBHW040134150726
48005CB00015B/2491